Dark cloud
White cloud
Dusk Sandstone
Volume 1

Paul Fearne

chipmunkapublishing
the mental health publisher

Paul Fearne

Published by
Chipmunkapublishing
United Kingdom

http://www.chipmunkapublishing.com

Copyright © 2018 Paul Fearne

ISBN   978-1-78382-403-8

There are times
In amongst the debris
That glean hope
And in these times
We are thankful
But what is there left
Of the tenderness of an autumnal day?
It is here
Where we shed our only desire

I have come for you
Oh hope
And there
Where we long to be
I have gathered a new beginning
That is more than we
Indeed
Had hoped

Be true, and then some
And the tide will swim in your favour
I am the thing that simply is
And here
Where we need a traveling mind
There will be recompense
And all that is left to give

The stark insistence of the way
Has born a mighty fruit
And when we are kind
It comes in sleep
We dream of it
And have our chance at interpretation
I feel the levity of all situations
That are my guides
That have wishing to be true

When we be
We compensate
Towards this
Or that

And when we find ourselves running
There will be time to rest

I know of no other thing
That is neither here
Nor there
I only know one thing
We are coming for the waiting
And all that is

I love what it is that I have become
In this there is no wager
I have read all the books
All the articles
And I am still here
Raining shards
And giving rank

Be something the world is not
And you will find a mighty source
I have want to think of things askew
And here find my release
But what do we have
But all that is
And all that will be

What do I find myself thinking
Of nature of course
And beauty
Yes beauty
It comes when you least expect it

The tenor of my argument is assured
I have read the greats
I have heard their superlatives
And now I know them to be true

A word of caution
We must live
And read
With pure passion
This much is true

I am the one who never gives in
Despite a loss of seemingly inordinate desperation
But onward we go
Never forgetting
What we set out to achieve

There are nuances in every journey
Even here
Between this nuance
And the next
There is time to gasp the air of the chosen

The sentience we feel in the sea
Is a great act
It turns us inward
And then lets us be

I feel now a sense of the new
New to start
And at every corner
Around we go

Whatever you are feeling now
Cannot be surpassed
It is in us not to see that
And when we hear
That life is too great
We must run to that chosen place
That allows no barbs

What I have been through
Knows only testament
But what there is
That is, is left
Is nothing other than all

I am feeling the weight lift from the shoulders of giants
They have come to pay salutations
And they know only what can never be true

Have heart
Steel your soul
And be prepared for the adventure
It will not stop
So brace yourself
Take the steel from your soul
And put it in your heart
Only give it when the time is right

What is more
There is a chance to be anew
Let the suffering you feel now
Be a riding force
That drives you onwards
And through
And to be the best of the best
And when you are done
There will be countless things to bring you back
Head them not
They are not of you now

The thing we most want from this existence
Is to flourish
And here seek a nesting place
High on the crags

The night time is what it is
We seek it
Because its fruit is one of persistence

I love what it is that we are
In reality we are something that tales cannot tell of
But what is the mainstay of it all?
A comedy that falls from the rooftops
And then is filled with life

The distance is fresh
But what of the night?
It is always here with us

There can only be what there is not
This seems a contradiction

But is not
When we are through reflecting
There will be love
And this love
This grand love
Will be more than we ever hoped

The test of things
Belongs to the fibres of our combined yearnings

I have felt
That when the bell is struck
The wind will be no more
And what we thought were our ancestors
Are more than we have ever dreamed of

I am coming for you fate
Brandishing the love I feel for all
I am your true friend
And that is all

The testament to this
Is that
What I feel
Has nothing of the base
And all of the immortal

I am want to be a stranger
In a strangeness
That has no levity
I have felt in the margins
What can only be called acceptance

Be the thing that barks
And you will be in the middle
Be the thing which has recourse to the stars
And your fate will be a lark

There is now no more in the wind
But it is here that we feel with most ardent passion

I like what I see
Do you?
This is not really a question
But a lesson learnt in full

What inspires me is nothing more than the light we have
At our disposal
Yes I am the thing that settles
I have not seen you yet
But in my time I will have many laughing's
And much more beside

I am the seeing when it is overcast
I am the one who says yes
Believe only one thing
Life is for the lark

I know that things will right themselves in the mist
Ah yes
The mist
It has come for us all
But what we further do not see
Is that the sea
Is all
And the harbour
Is where we are at

There can only be what is
There can only be all
What is there
Is there
What is left
Has the mark of all

I hear you
In your time of need
But that is not enough
You must straddle the four horses
Of the apocalypse
And ride them on
To greater things

I feel your need
But remember
When the light burns the brightest
There will be more than we have ever hoped for

The timing of this
Is perfection in every sound
I long to this results
But the silence is all I have

The tempest has us all
And what we know of it
Is left to the ancients

I am like the wind
That stirs the clouds
I have a gauge
That time has yet to embrace

Will you be with me in this journey?
It is an adventure of mighty proportions
Yes
Adventure
That is the key
Belief in adventure
We can indeed believe

I hear you
When you say
You cannot see the ear of things
But what I say
Is yes
We will conquer

In the distance
Between this rainbow
And the next
There will be time
To gather up our thoughts
And send them to the other shore

Paul Fearne

I am here
Where the sandpiper sleeps
I have found all that can be
And know
That the wind will be a keepsake

There are now things that keep the sand
Away from my toes
The sea keeps the beach
As a watchmen keeps the time
I have found you, oh life
And know you to be a treasure

What will become of the sky?
She is here with us
And there will more of her than ever
To see her brilliance

I have come for the daylight
And I have found its delight
Be true
The messenger says
And ring the bell
There can be nothing more than this

There are chances that breed new adventure
But what is most at stake
Is the narrowness of the aperture
There is more, as there is less

I will use my plight
To gather new folds
Folds in the seam of things
And here
Where the distance between the tethers that bind
Is enough to shrew the happenstance
Into mountainous deliverances

Have a hold on things
As we all must
And there will be a chance
To once again

Be that thing with might
Might and happiness
I like

Things come
And things stay
What do we say
When the moon is at its apogee?
Does it ever get there?
It is forever

Yes, forever
There are things I wish to say
And I will say them
Before it is too late

Writing is like the dance
And the dance is in the well
And the well is in the mist

The chance we have to mind ourselves
Is now here
And we will take it

What is more
I have life
It flows in me
And then I will come
And know this life to be more than I have ever known

Things stir
And things alight
And when we are done
That is it
No more of the round
No more of the cavalcade
Only
What can never be explained

The things we must do while the embers burn
Are enough to keep us

And here
Where the gleaning mass
Keeps nothing
I will find the newness of a fading sun
And there
In the mist
Treasures to overcome

I like what I see
I wonder in time
And belief
And all that is sourced from the upright
I have not known the trees to be so green
But what of their greenness
I am here

This much is true
There will be a breeze to catch
And a wondering at the magnificence of it all

Be the thing that bites
And there will be recompense
Be true
In this life
And you will win a mighty release

I have found myself in the midst
Of a mighty battle
And I know who will win

Draw feathers in your sketch book
And the time it takes to be a fighter
Will be yours

Fight for the wind
Fight for life
Fight for your need to be
And there will be
More than can be

I have heard it said
That life is a nuance

Dark cloud White cloud Dusk Sandstone Volume 1

That life is a meaning
That life is
And simply is

I come for the night
I come for the day
But which do I prefer?
Even more so!

Evening time stretches
And evening time marches
But in the end
Both is required

The listening the twilight does
To fill our hearts with marvels
Is nothing more than we should expect

I dare you to live!
And we will!

I have never be one to shy from the fight
Only because I know what is at stake
I will be the one who loves
Only because I miss the attention

I need something more
Which I have found
But the travesty of us all
Burns deep

I long to be that thing which is found
But that is not the sense I have at order
I love the muse
And she loves me
Should I even write that?
We'll let it be

There can never be a thing that holds
In this world of ours
Only a thing that harbours

As if too late

I will emulate the grandeur of the horizon
And here be what most say is true
I will write from truth
And know this to be a starting point

The conditions are set
The time is right
The newness of a fading light
Are already met

But what of the night?
She burns in us
And knows what is best
Is here already

I come to sail away
To that misty clime
It will keep the birds at bay
And shimmy like a willow

I have heard it said
That nothing ever comes of this
But what I know is different
Like wastrels in the water

I know that when we are through
There is mystery
I have my theories
But how many are true?

The difference in the speed of things
Is like a mighty envelope
That dins
As it elopes

What of the mastermind
Who has his hat tipped?
We will see
Before we are pipped

'All writing must be clear'
Never a poet did hear
'All writing is pale'
That will start a gale!

In the mean time
I will jest
I will find it more
And sometimes less

What have we said
Other than all?
What have we cried
Other than the small?

There will be times amongst this
To tell of fortunes bell
And all that will come to pass
And nothing here of hell

Be true
I have said it before
But it warrants more
For it is the key

What have we now?
What fresh mint the smell of which
Leaves languid cushion
On fettered brow?

I have seen the mark
And read the shrew
Of makers name
And remedy through

Be a class
I have had my say
I know not what
Keeps you at bay

Dreaming in the mist
I have had my say
Be what may
I will not delay

What is this
I hear you say?
It is the cast of thousands
That lingers nightly
By my grave
Oh, how spritely

Be the track
Of all that is wholesome
And you will find
More than you are holding

Come to the bastion
Of want and pleasure
It is a firm thing
To be measured

What we say
Is that the clouds are waning
And the dreams are palling
And the dregs are sailing
Happiness to us all!

I know of no other way
I am mired in feelings that have no want
I am seeking deliverance to where?
I know that this sounds odd
But I must write
Or be shod

The testament to my face
Is the rancour in the rails
It seems so hard to be
And finds the lifeless
In me

Dark cloud White cloud Dusk Sandstone Volume 1

There are things in the sky
That only have themselves to be with
Here we run anew
And know that
When the dawn has had its way
There will more time for rejoicing

Love and habit
They sleep
In separate beds
They lull
And be seen with more

To chose
Is to live
We have choices
And know not which way to look

Be standing
And be attuned
To all that is

There will come time for us
To be the ones who last
I don't know what I am doing
But will try again

Here
The levity is like a show
It sends us deep
And yet still swimming

The noise in here is harsh
But there can be no other way
I am like I should be
And that is more like the dawn

See what is more
And what is less
That is my signature
Of this place

Paul Fearne

And the rest

Why do I ramble so?
It is not in me to say
I am blessed with this
And that
They hold me
I suffer for them
I will not rest
Until I am done
The fortitude that holds me
Holds me still
I am still
And still breathing
Here there is nothing more
Than all

The tariff of the world
Is with us
It bends and stretches the seams of things
And when we think all is aright
It comes again
And again

The distance I find between each star
Is like my furthest homely wish
I have not seen another
Who has washed a similar dish

The sense I have that we
Will be okay in the night
Is like a mantle that pours its sickly web
Into chalices of another

I sense in the weave of things
That the night cannot hold me

I have often thought
By the light of the things that steel
That newness of the spring will solve all

Dark cloud White cloud Dusk Sandstone Volume 1

The genealogy of fate
Has me here
What is done, can be nothing more than all

I see you now, oh spring
It is all I ever wanted
I will whisper to you
And know your reply

What is more, I will only bend
In the right frame
And in the right nuance

I have seen it
It is true
The life I led was full of the condition
But you were lending
A helping hand
To your fellow
But let us just be friends now
It is over

I wish I had a hand that never shook
No I don't
I love it
It makes me who I am
A levity around the margins

Consigned to that which only lasts
I set my sights for the rest

But what of life?
It is here
And there
And roundabouts
There is one thing for sure
Dukkha

But how do we overcome it?
With steel
And certainty

And all that is

Be a fawning
And light will be your curve
I have led many adventures
And I hope for more

What have I felt, but all
I have known the kingdom
And the sand
And all that lies in between

Some have said
I am a gallivanter
But I know my trade

There is sense
Where
There is nothingness
There is life
In them hills

Every line
Sings a song
And every destiny
Loves its ilk

The things which bind
Are the same things release
Lo
All we must do is look

The further I go into this
The further from the nest I go
Is there wishes in the wind
Please

The forest is dark
As the time for life is vociferous
I catch myself at the brink
Is this what I want?

Then, in the glade
A light
But let me set the scene
Dark cloud
Light cloud
Dusk
Sandstone
This much is certain
An ancient university begins in this glade
This much is certain

What do I say to you
Oh life?
Can we ever be in tune?

The listening that the sands do
Is more of this
And less of that
And here
We should part

The distance I have travelled for this
Is more than I have ever hoped for
You are the one I seek
And now that we are there
We must share a solemn oath

The likeness of my mother
I send the tune a bleeding
And when the time has passed
I listen to you, heading

The sentience in the hills
Is more than a mouthful
And here
I will take the wind
And know it to be a thing of purpose

What do you say to that, old man?
I will always be yours, as you are mine

The tinkle of the sound
Is like a harsh gushing of effect
Where in the middle of our boat
Four oars sit stranded
The oasis we seek is not of this sea
But where we justify ourselves
In the name of the daffodil
I seek recompense

The liking I have of more
Is nothing other than loss
Be in the windswept
And I will be yours
Be true
Be true

What have I left?
And still it goes
I have fought the fight
And I am left now
With the incomparable
Be true
Be true

The sentience we feel
Is a long lost soldier
He hurries in from the cold
And releases his story
I am one to bark here
Not because I can
But because I must

There are well-springs of relief
That know of no other way
Except here
And there

Where will we be to
In the vacuum of salience?
There are choices to me made
And all in good time

I love the house in which I was born
There is only one photo of it with me in it
And that photo is now love
And all it can bring

I listen intently to the sound of the sea
And here, where I hear
I loose myself
Magnificent cathedral
Stirrings of other worlds
Chastisements from a great teacher
I love you now
As I always have
But when we parted
I lost the base
And slid into oblivion
Can I call you 'love'
One last time
You will ignore me
But that is okay
I swim
And make noise
Like all good writers should
But where is the destiny I knew to be great?
It is here
In all the life we were assured of
In the dark
I lunge for homely aphorisms
How many words are there exactly?
We will never know

In the listings I have your nearness
They are a faint away
From the newness of the flight
I am whisked
Is that the right word
Whisked?
It matters little now

Coming from the outside of the rhythm
I will be base

Paul Fearne

Instead of truly base
There is a likeness to the crow
As it stands in stark reminder
I feel your cold
As my cold
You will never know these words
But I will!
And that is all that matters

Seeing is what we see here
Seeing is the tentacle of what lies
Inside
This much I can say

The testament to light
As all good things
Is in the wind
I cannot to begin
I will always begin

I have read enough to sink any ship
And then
You know what
I stopped reading
I once knew a poet
Who didn't read poetry
All this is with us

I am the flag on the mast
I am he that makes no sense
And when we are through
There will come a mighty peace
Believe you me

I will elevate you
On the pinions of desire
They are here now
Waiting

I have sought
All the truisms of the land
And when we are here

Dark cloud White cloud Dusk Sandstone Volume 1

I will tell you
And be placated in my state

There is a place
That has no bounds
In it
Lye the shards of autumn light

There are mists
That tarry no longer
There are strangers
That have no fear
I liken the semblance of the stars
To your face

What is here
Is yet to come
What is moisture on the clouds
Is not enough to rain

The silence I feel
When we have all been together
Is like that rock
The carries
Through the ages

What we see
When the sea
Is at an end
We see
More
Than we ever could

The treasuring we do
To keep the squall
At bay
Is enough to fathom a mountain
In all that can be found

A truth is an annual
Of all that is

But when the sequence leads to vitriol
There is never enough

Fly free
Oh soul
You will find new ground
And new places to be

I have here now
All that I need
To be in the window
Of the feeling of content

There are just so many pieces of this puzzle
That I cannot believe in one
There are chances at the daylight
I will always take

The insistence is here
Like fire on ice
But there are no real threats
Only entreaties

The longed for place
Is where I wish it to be
Home
And light
And all that is

Have you seen it?
This merry ride
It is enough to be what it is now
A companion to the stars

I have felt the newness of the sun
On my fate
And here
Where the wings of desire have faulted
I will believe

The testament to the wandering
Is never more than now

I hear your song
But know it to be
A keepsake of proportions

The deepest part of me
Has found what it is
That keeps us ticking
But I will not let on
I know it to be knowledge
And them some

The wish I once had
To carry away
Firefly's
To their ancient home
Is where I am now
But with a difference
I will go with them

Be the one who sighs
And the mountains will clear a pass for you
Be the one who does not feel
And there will be a neat surprise

I see you now
The one in the mirror
I love what it is
That keeps us free
I am like the sense in between the nonsense
And here
Where the loading mass of ripe disregard
Is at its utmost peak
I will be here
And never there

Come to the distance
And you will find
More than you ever have hoped
There is more
And here it will be
In the mist

Paul Fearne

And through

Never again
Will I sigh
Never again
Will I be in the line of sight
Never has the sea so much hope for me
Never has the land seemed so close
When we reign
We reign only a short time
And then fate plays her hand
And that is all

The mischief of the trees
Is not enough to stop us
I hear your call
But know of no other way
Maybe this is just
How it is supposed to me

This is what we find
When we search the bottom of things
A new hope
A new way to be

I care not for the departed
Here is where it is at
And when the nuances
Of a worn out soul
Are here in the midst of things
I will find more
Than I ever have

What is more
There is more
To say
And less
Depending on which side of the coin
Drops first

What we have come for
Is nothing more than all

But what we now need
In the hallow which is our soul
To be freed
And sent back to us
Via the dams of acceptance
And all that is (rosy fingered dawn)

The healing I come for
Is not what I expected
Put I will utilise its passion
And see it as nothing less
Than what I do, indeed, need

Feathers
Of autumn light

When the clearing has us
We must let go
Of all of this
And that
And see it for a wanting need
And the glass floor
Of the world
As it is

What do you do
When sight is at hand
We draw our feather
And have it hold the dream aloft

And when there is no more
There will be room
And them some

What is this?
I ask you
It is nothing other than all
And everywhere we look
Lo, it is found
Come now
There can be no more

Paul Fearne

Of this or that
Or flight
Or acceptance

The shirt is off the back
The need we have is here
There can only be one thing that sides
With us now
And that is dew on the grass
During a spring morning

There is now a place for me
Amongst the treasury of the beyond
I hear its call
And know that the semblance of the night
Will not have me

Be the one who thinks
And the distance will not matter to you
This is what we are here for
No matter what

I am thinking myself
Of things that have only themselves
In this way
I write
And know my words
To be treasures of feeling

The beauty of it all
Don't the poets always have rhapsody
Over it
Don't we all forget ourselves
Over it
Why did Plato hold his thought
Over poet's?
There is no telling

I have a new thought
One that rings in the ears
Before it is cast off
It tells

Dark cloud White cloud Dusk Sandstone Volume 1

Of truncated rhythms
Of old and small

But what do we think of the rest?
It is hard to say
The daylight will come
And then we may rest

What is this before me?
It is the wind
And the rain
And all that will come to pass

I have never been one to run
Because here
There is fortitude
Like nothing we have seen before

What is more
There is a chance of new beginnings
As she reigns
On shards of silk

Be my wanting
And I will only forget

For the time being
There is beauty
But beauty has a limit
I will extend that limit
And see what is there

Foraging
In the margins
I know my place
To be one that waits
I am a writer
But that is only
Winkling in starry night

Be what can only be termed
Water
And sense will always prevail

I listen closely
And that is all

What do we say
When the curtain call
Begs to differ?
We say yes
That is all

But despite this
We need that special embrace
That tarries long
As it does hard
There is here
A nuance
That defies the mould
But do not be concerned
Trenches will fight the stitches

What can be more true
Of this life
Than the outside
We look in
And through
And have our vestiges come for complaining
The tempest is here
As always
But what we seek now
Is something in the seam of things
It tarries
As we all do
But now
In the thick of it
There are trees growing
The fabled mass of intemperance
Speaks to a weary heart
Forgive, and be done with it

Dark cloud White cloud Dusk Sandstone Volume 1

The touch of the other
Is not the same
As the dawns light
They are similar
But the dawn can only imagine
Where the other loses sight
What is beauty?
I have said my piece
But here
Where languishing stars have their sway
I need to know one thing
Is there this
Or that?
I will know
On the last great adventure
Some have had their say
And this is mine
Granting half of human endeavour
There is a steel that binds
And here we have
The last great adventure

The teething of the mass
Is endured before we have had our say

I clutch at sticks
But have my turn to say
What will become of us
When the silent museum
Is here?

There are never warbling's so dear
As we are about to say

This is the might
As it is the power
Be a vacuum
And you might win

The tempest
Yes
Can there be any stronger thing?

What have I thought
But all
What have I landed
But what is not

Now, when we see ourselves for the first time
Now, when the compass has not the need
Is it not now, that we see ourselves
For the last time
And always

The question lingers
But where is the bight?
It is here
In this very shadow
And as I have no questions
I will away
And then return
For the penultimate
And then more

Here we are then
In the midst of things
Things that never do away with
And only then arise

There is a new art
In every fibre
It comes in sand
And all that transpires
I love the silk
That has wheat
As it does
Chaff
And here
Where the windows renege
There is a mist
That has no time

It feels itself to be true
And then runs
That solemn mile
To the sea
And here
Where thunder
Brings the terror of the sublime
There will be lots to talk of
Now and again

What is left?
There is one thing
That knows neither bow
Nor arrow
It is the gist of things to come
And in the middle
Of this to-ing
And fro-ing
Is the light that guides
Here
Where the sun can no longer shout
There is a what-for
That has as its base
The dreams of larger men

Be me
There is nothing left to say
My suffering is nowhere hidden
It is like the tempest that has no blast
It is the well-spring that gives no release
And here
Where the fathoming of angels
Are like the recipe for the fight
I will cling to you
And say I am here

But what is it we say
That makes it all go away?
There is nothing to be said here
Only listening with divine teeth
And here

Where the stall to action is a never ending fall
That leads only backwards
And through
Come and be the way
There will be a story to tell afterwards
This much is true

What is more
Is not that the sun will not last
And
That the traipsing through the inner
Is not at odds with the sea
But rather
The whole established enterprise
Is at a sea
So over blown
That to walk under it
Is to feel fate

There comes a time
When sentience cannot last
And in that time
There is a mighty rejoicing
Rejoicing for the release
Of pens un-mighty
Be here oh worth
You are the sea
As I am the wandering
There can be no time now
That does not find shelter
And that does not find the trail
Of worn down disaster
And all it does not entail

What have we here?
It is the sand
As it is the tears
Lost in the longest breath
There will come a time for sailing
And a time for being elated
The treasure that you now see
Has long been shackled to the stars

And they will take her
Before too tong

Then
And now
There is the show of stallions
They breathe a mighty cold breath
And have stones for eyes
And know their roundedness to be a blessing
What is more
There can be only hope here
Only what is most aside from happiness
They have the chortle

Steaming forth
I renege to write
From nothing other than the nib
And here
Where the beauty has me still
I am longing for the festooned and the savy
Be calm
Things will come

Be sure
I am not the one to enter
Such a castle as this
I am like the saving life
Which curtails as it lunges

And here
Oh hear
There are new surprises
That have only tempests that dine
And in the movement of the soul
A new feasting replenishes
I like what I see
And hear what I see
Also

In the meantime
I must not be mean

There must be levity
As gracious as the next
And here
Where folds of time
Know no grace
There is a lassoing
That heads
As it spoils
The sombre
And the blind
What is more there can never be enough
Of this
And that
And the temptation to be more than we should
·Is here
With the stallions of time
This will stir
But I have no choice
Choices are not in the way
They are with the weather

Hasten to the brink
There is more time now than ever
And when we see aright
There will be nothing left to see
And here
Where embers of midnight dancing
Are still to be foiled away
There will come a romance that truly is
And have no more of the faux
True romance
That does not hide its face
That does not here itself aloof
There will be more of this
Than we have ever seen before
And then onwards
To the centre of it all
And here we will know peace
And all that is

What is more
I must not rest

Not for this place
Not for the next
And here
Where the dandelions
Have had their say
There will enter the newness of it all
And we will know
That times spent in tempest
Are at the right pitch to be
And here
Where longing bends its bow towards forever
There will be a travelling destiny
That has only wishing as its base
And not anything as it wants to be

We have here
What cannot be
We have here
What has always been
And when we come
To be in tune with the rest
There will be an utmost relief
Come to guide us
And then to be the one
Who heals

Be free, I hear you say
Be the never before seen applause
And with that
Simply be
That much I have been
To those who chose to stay
And those who were thirsty
See a preparedness
For the wanting of us all
And it will be there

What do we say here
When rain has had its final insistence?
I do not know
And here

Where the meadows long to tread
And the discs of sunlight yearn to be
There will be hallowed turf
Sitting beside us
And through
And then what of the rest?
There can be more
Only when we let it
I like this noise
It is the noise of ages
It sings a song that is not heard anywhere else
But only on the stairs leading to nowhere
Do we hear it

Can we be more than we want?
Yes
And no
And all that is

Be the merriment of the stars
And your life will be full
Be the insistence of the world
And you will be full beyond measure

I have had my fill of these things
And it is only now
That I lose myself in time
And time enough
Be the happiness of the trees
And you truly be free
Be what comes for fate
And life will be yours

When we say our last word
Here
Where there is nothing more
We find peace
And here
Depending on our lives
We find that true form
That knows only rest

And now for something more
In the density of condolences
There lives
And breathes
The ancients
And all their wisdom
I come for you
People of old
I come for that which is more than the hammer
I come for that which is more old than the old
I simply come
And then believe once again
In the testament of love
A book we should all carry

What is hard
Is hardest
Is these words
Is these words and more
And more than these words
And all that should be

What do you think, think of all this
It is the belief of a rain-soaked umbrella that guides me
Do not be ashamed
There is nothing to be ashamed about
Only the dirt we leave
When we have lived

What do we say
When times are good?
We look back with a certain fondness
And know that lives have been crossed
And adventures have been had

This is what I say to you
To the near and far
I say, be true
And your lives will be incumbent
Of all the wealth of this world
And the next

And now, is a final saying
I have the trace
And you can have it too

I have longed for more
I have found
More
But what is missing
Is not the piece
Of the long lost puzzle
But more of what we say
Is fine

Be the thing that says
And you will be rewarded
Be headed for the castle
And we will come with you
There are no more whistlings
To be with us
But that is okay
We will mark time

Where is it written
That the tool is found in the spark?
I have written mostly on bark
And here
Where the sound of longing is now forever being found
I will come for you
And I will see you getting back
And I will ask two questions
And afterward, tip my hat to you

And know your forest to be deep
I have not lost you
Only found you
That time again
And again

What do we dream of
This sound of ours?
We dream of sleep
And all that can be

Be sure
I will be the one who laughs
I am taking the long road
For the short road is taken
And here
Where the mist is no longer the sand
I will cover you
With a tenderness
That knows only silk

What do we
When to do
Is no longer?
We gather ourselves
And be like the truisms
We write of
Yes
I must write of the feeling we have
But this is not enough to quench us
But only enough to cool us

Be the one who laughs
And we will all laugh
I have known of many things
And I have laughed at many things
And here
Where the distance is not an eyesore
But a lesson learnt through time
I will catch thee
And know thee to be a traveller too

But what is beauty?
It is where the home has its greatness mystery
But in the longing we have
There is change
And all is called to be
And be again
Not before too long
At least

Paul Fearne

Now I see you
Loud and clear
And when I know your name
I will have both my hands
To shake yours
And we will be friends
And reminisce about bygone times
And have lamps as companions
And know their light to be good

What do we see?
When to see
Is to step
On infirm ground
Do we continue?
Yes
We must
And then
Be in tune with the longing of clouds
As they spill from heaven's tent
Be rent
And then create

There is never enough
No
This is not quite true
We must look a little deeper
And yes
We will come to what is closest to us

What is this?
I hear you ask
It is more than we had ever hoped for
And here
Where sound is not in the movement of the world
But the tightness of its joints
We will come
And know ourselves to be stronger than any sound
But on this firmament
Nor any other

What do we say to ourselves
When the trend is in the right
We lie face down
And have our new need righted

Be alive again
There will be more to come
There are needs we have
That have not been met for an age
But what is this?
That bends around us
It is here again
In our arms
I like the things which yearn
The things which have a life
The things that we cannot let go of
I see the right aright
But do not wish to take part
I love the sands as they are
And come the hidden way
I will believe once again

It is like no other sound
This sound of ours
It is like we never were
And here
Where the bull
Is off the chain
I will come for you
In the most mightiest of forms
Known to this brethren
Or that
Be a life giver
Not a life taker
And you will see your error
I am like the former
In the later
I am like the bird
In the nest
I have seen your way
A thousand times

Again and again
I will see your smile
And that will be enough

What do you fear?
When the night comes
There is no respite

But maybe there is
I will have things in the hereafter
That do not say their name
Be true
And you will fight a lovely fight
It will be soft to the tug
And more than that

Adjacent to the façade
Is that which will not reside
We love its nuances
And hear its voice

What is that which has tears?
It is the wandering of fireflies
In dead of night
It is the rhapsody of laughter
That sings through the night
And has us as the lasting grace
Of this and other times and places

I will not linger one second
More than is accomplished by fate
There will be the singing of something new
And something old
And all that will be
In the coming down of strangers

Be what may
I will conquer
Like none have done before
And here
Where the nuisance
And levity

Have a co-mingling
I will banish thought
And just act
And here be happy with myself
And know myself to be the envelope
That has no aperture
No thing to read out loud

I need no further reluctance
Than what is here
Be still
It suits us all

I am now in my youth
And here I hear you say
I will be in my youth for years

Be the treasure
And I will be the hearth
We are there to be
You and I
I will remember
This time
As perhaps my greatest

There are motions now
That have no wheelings
There are destinations
That believe no truth
But in the wind
There is a found thing
It loves the treasures of our spines
And works with wonder over our knees

I sit
And watch the world
It is a machination of insouciance
That has us dreaming

I love it now
As it has no treasure

Paul Fearne

I love it
As all things
I will wind down
Only when it is time to stop
And here
Oh here
There will be rest

I have felt the sand
Between your fingers
And here
Is where the distance
Never matters
I will love you never the less
Despite our parting
I will seek redress
From the clouds
And know them
For the first time

Will you linger
And then sing your song?
I hope it is a tune
Of utmost insistence

Be the thing that belies fate
And the dance will not be a stranger
In a strange land

There are always things to do
But we must do them
And do them we well

The newness of a fading kiss
The afterglow of tomorrow
We will sing
Until singing is no longer
I will yearn for you
Only because I can
I will send seams
To seamless places
I will beckon only the erudite

To sing with me

Do not be afraid
It is not me who is laughing
I hold onto such thoughts
As a man at sea
A man at sea
But who breathes
And feels his weight
Only
From time to time

I come for the need
But stay for the lack
I believe once again in the straightness of time
I follow
And be aware
I love the chase
But what of the night?
You are the one who seeks
But I am the one
Who does not fear
Your love is like the window
It sees beyond
And into deliverance
I have gathered myself a new feeling
It is the one I left behind at the start
Of this mighty adventure
I have no cavort to send me
I have only flowers
That seek the dream in night

There are too many things
That are said by the waylaid
They know who is in the sense
And who is the senseless
Be what may
I will continue

What is the way
I hear you say?

It is forward
It is backward
It senses the need we have
To fathom back a little
And then up
And around

Do not tempt me
Mighty ruler
I am one for the song
But not one for the party

I tread on silk
And know it to be glass
I sink to new heights
But have height as an advantage

The beauty of the place
Was no lost on me
In me
And through me
I have thought
That times are enough to be treasured
And here again
Where we believe
There is a chance to live again
Without fear
Of loss
Or fortitude

I hear what you say
But I am here to be
And that is what I will do
And that is all that I will say on the matter

The closer we get to the slope
The more speed we accumulate, and then
Down we go
Through the many peaks and troughs

I wish I was here with the rest
But this is not what I have achieved

And here, I will sing
And sing again

There are chances that do not sing
There are occasions that do not riddle
I have found the way
And know it to be a thing of truth
But what of this setting
That beats a drawing constancy
There is nothing left to see
Only settle in time
And be what we may

The time I have in my pocket
Is not the time of the world
It is something new
That has no need of the old
Be the tempest
And I will love you
Be the lyre
And time will be yours

What is it you say?
I have never known fate?
But I have my dear
I have
She has been that which takes me
To all four corners
Of man's dissolution on the wind
Be the tempest
And I will blast
Be the way we used to be
And I will never sway again

I have been the in between of things
But this is only my calling
A calling I take seriously
And know how to settle

What is this
In the middle of things?

It is the one true
The one thing that does not bite

I have heard it said
That we should not disturb the living
But what is this but a dream of silk
There is much fibre that has as its substance
A more envisaged dimension
Be assured
There is nothing left to give
It has all been given
And given in such a way as to be glass
Coloured glass
Of the most beautiful dimensions
I have travelled the road that is here
And known it to be chaste
And here
I will know peace
And never be righted

What are the things which stay?
Everything, it seems, goes
But in the meantime there is something more to do
I have led my life to utmost sincerity
And what is my reward
What I wanted of course
A bit of this
And a bit of this
When will I be?
I ask myself
In the fullness of time
This is sure

The next time I stipulate an adventure
Can we do it in halves and not in yokes
There is here something to be said
And we will say it
Maybe next time

Have we the chance to say
That everything is alright
That things will right themselves

For the tempest to depart
And the niceties to come again

What is this thing we say
When we cannot say anymore?
It is the same as the winter
And all that is in
The shards of the walking mass

Be the one who says more
And there will be the chiming of the day
Be that which we know
And there will be more to say

I have said once again
Be true
And this much will be the beginning

Have you seen
The latest desire?
It is here with us now
But will we pursue it?
Yes and no
That is the way to deal
With all our woe
And here
Were we sleep again
There will be more to tell of
Than ever before

What is there to say
When all has been already said?
There can only be the thing that belies
And in this
Be a troubadour
Of things to see
And things to be

There are many new faces here
They list on unhappy places
But in the meantime

Paul Fearne

There is a likening to the stars
That have their fate
And have their way to be

I am the newest of the lot
And know that time cannot hasten me
Be the one that tries to be
And you will be the one
Who comes to ride the steed of trembling ease
And this will be enough
To make dreamers of us all

The sense we all make
In the morning's light
Is enough to be the thing
Which raises us from the brink
And has us lie down
Until we sleep no more
Be kind here
There is no sight

I feel the wind
It comes before me
And I raise it up
To be free at last
And off it goes
Like timbre in a forest
The storm
It bends
But not too far
Nor too short

Be in line with things
They will not be vanquished
Nor headed by any venom
In the sentience of the dream
There is more to harbour
In the litany of the senses
There are places to find help

The newness of the listening
Is here before us

And when we seek the hearsay
Of the longing
It will be here
This much is certain

What do you say
When dreams are made of laughter?
We do not say much
But carry on
Regardless

 What do you say to me
When all is here and done?
You say words of sweet aplomb
And dervish accolades
That have no sense
Nor time to reason

Be with me now
Oh fates!
The time is upon us
And we must accomplish
Before it is the latest of tributes
A song for the ages
A winters that eases still
And all that
Will come to pass

What is there beneath
That doesn't come a beat?
What do we know
That stills us, and then?
I have felt the fire of thine eyes
And of thine speech
Wishing like deliverance
To all that will come to pass

Have the sense to say nonsense
And have the trapsidaisical at your heed
Do more than that
And you will stay

What's more
You will have light
From your fingers
And farrowed brows
To your wanting

In the sign along the way
There is a space
In that space is the world
In this world
Are you and me
As we look at the sign along the way
Where there is a space
Etc

Be the sense of things
They will travel
To higher reaches
And then find their way down again
And through things
We have only dreamed about
Knowing this
I will say
Yes
We are free

What do we run for?
It is to steel our soles
And let them be the honour
Of those who need

The ones who need
Are the ones who share
Are the ones who navigate
With never ending might
The ones who listen
And the ones who bite

What have we to gather
For ourselves?
It is everything that whims
And everything

That ever
Was

In the dreaming we do
To further the need we have
There is such poignancy
That it is hard to forget
But when we are done
And we are left with our dreams
Here we return
To that most ardent adventure
One that has life as its base
And systems of emancipation
As her truth

What I long for most of all
Is the key to be used
To break me open
And let the farrow height
Be in tune
With all that is

I am left with the thought
That travels nearly as far as I
That the sense we see in things
Is an illusion
And all is a show
We have paid handsomely to see

Come to me in the midst of things
There will be a wager
Who is it that will conquer
The winner, or the loser?
I know you have the time
As I have the need
I know you are the one
That I see in my former self
What is there to say
But the horror
Will heal all

Be the testament
And it will rain
Come and see the sights
Instead
And see where they take you

I have found a way to be induced
From this birth
Towards the infinite
And here, where things seem good
I will be the one who says yes
And then go from there

This noise
Is not what we are carrying
It is something more
And something less
In the together
That is the trumpet of the day

What have we got
But all that is?
I hear your song
And know it to be true
And when you venture
Out into the wild
You will not be one to shirk
But one to travel in harmony
Towards so much
And through
So little

There is now something we must do
We must go forward into the mist
And here find our own sense
Of the right
And here
Be willing to be
Until there is nothing left
Of the sharp and bulbous
Of the deafening and the quick
Be true

I will say it again before we are through
Be true
That is all

I have found a way through
It is in these words that I write to you
And here
Where the semblance of the systematic
Is aligned with beauty
Here I will find you
And all that you are

There is more to say than this
And all that is will suffice
I have come many miles
To see you here
And when I finally see you
I will know you to be true
What is more
That which comes with you
Into the daylight
Will not fathom your mysteries
In an afternoon
Or then some
Be what may
We will see the next
In the next
And be thankful that we are ready to something new
And then

 Be the tenacity
And I will be your guide
Be the withstanding
And there will be things to write about
I know
That in the harbour
That carries these shores
There will be
Mighty festivities
That can have only the time that is spent
On this applause

And that irrepressible insistence
And here
Where we shout the loudest
We will win a mighty battle
And feel worthwhile again

There is here
A standing that belies all
In it
There is shed
A light
That remembers its own birth

And here
Where milk runs like honey
There conditions a mighty semblance
Of desires unseen
Of things not yet tried
Where the sense of the senseless
Is meadowed in tribes of happenstance
There comes a feathering
And a new found freedom
In all
And like happenings in the sky
That give more
Than we'd hope

What have we left
Of all our rambling?
We have the measure to suit
And the seams are on the cusp
Be the languid charm
And there will be more than can be occupied with
Be what may
There will never be enough

Desire
And all her ilk
Are laden with the basket
Of the fabled and the beautiful
But always look
Before you proceed

Dark cloud White cloud Dusk Sandstone Volume 1

Time has a way of processing
What should only be said

There are times we must forget
And times we will not forget
There is only one thing that says with any certainty
I will give until giving is no more
And here
Where we creep so carefully
We see ourselves in the winnowing nest
Where birds have their rest
And humans face their faces
Be the one who laughs
And there will be merriment all round
And everything we must see to is carried away
Like a carriage before the ocean
We see it
And pledge always to ride
Or let run free
Here is the mystery
And the pulp of it

When the sense we have fails
There will be time for the laughter
Of a thousand nights labour

I will follow things through
And know that when the tenderness
Of a seemingly ancient
Togetherness
Is near at hand
I will be the one who has the sense

I feel now
Stronger than I ever have
It seems
As though the dust is a miniature
And the conch is a blessing

There are times
When we should not shirk

Paul Fearne

There are times when we must live
And in living
Feel the wroth
Of all that is

In the middle of a dreaming sleep
I awake
To find myself anew
There can be no pleasure greater than this
And when we spark
We find ourselves treasured
Like a new born
And then given licence to pursue

I will find the weather
To my liking
And know that
When things are calm
Here I am

In the meantime
There are things
That do not harness
They travel
As travellers in autumn light
I love what it is
That sees me so
I have to work out
What it means to be
I have to be sure
That things will right themselves
What have I to write about
But all that is
And here
Where I belong
I will come for you
Oh life
And be placated

There is still in the weave
A fabric that is tactile
And lets us be as we want

Dark cloud White cloud Dusk Sandstone Volume 1

What I caution you
Is not in the saying
But in the dreaming

Here we come again
And again
And there is more than ever
To soothe
As to bend
And then
Once again
To be as we like
Chose the best path
And you will find love
And then again
Life and togetherness

What I thought
Was gone
Was only a misconception
Of the dreams we have
For this
And for that

And here
Where our dreams are at their height
I will come for something more
Something to tender the lamps
In all their motion
And be true to what is

I have felt
That what is more
Is never enough
There are times
In the mainstream of things
That can reverberate
With ever increasing delight
And here
I will stay
To do my work

Paul Fearne

And the work of others

My tune
Is one of harvest
It embitters me to send the sake
Of all that is
Towards the sea
For I will find it there
And know it to be a thing of the well

You are the nightingale
As I am the sense
You are the window
That looks upon the raging sea
I will start again
Until all that is left of me
Is a corridor in the heart

You are sure
As I am late
You are here
As I am there

I have often thought
That the ties that bind
Are the same
As the ties that loosen
Allowing the world
To revolve
And then let go

I have found
In all my wanderings
A sense amongst the dysphoria
It is here
Like milk
Only to be set upon
By the ardent

There can always be time
Time to heal
Time to relax

And then….
Amazement!

What do we call
But all that is
What do we say
But yes!

I have never known this
In the double of the sound
There is a working wind
It knows how to be liked
When it wants to be
But here
Where the sound of frivolity echoes
I will continue
And know myself to true

What do we say
We the overcast bastion
Leaves its unruly nest
We say
Yes!
And then
Have at our beck
The seeds of a larger turning

What have we too say
When the landmark
Of our wanderings is silk
And the tempest that brought us
Oh so fickle

What do we say
When the tension between
This insistence and the next
Is a fathomable distress
That belies the temperature of the mass

I am the one who seeks
And the one who lives

Paul Fearne

But in the meantime there is revelry
And a chance to be delivered

I will hang my hat
And know it to be well at hand

I have found amongst the debris
A place to live
A place to be
And a place to rest

Some call the land we live in
A Newstead
I call it a place to be
A place to live
And create

This is the key for me
A place
I have long been a wanderer
And my fathoming tool
The words I write
Are my companions
On this journey of mine

There are times I wish you were here
When the dance was at its height
I wish
Oh I wish
That the semblance of the dance
Was a dance
To be enthralled

I have found
That this enticement
Is the one I am with
I love the swallow at dawn
I love the sea at dusk
And here
Where the new feeling
Is at its peak
I wish

And wish
For the dance

I long for the newness of a fading light
Of the chance to swim in the river of new found dreams
I see you now
You seem happy
We were once amazing
But that can never be undone
I have found my niche
And I exist
But to live
Again
That would be grand

The silence I have not heard in a while
Is neither here nor there
There are trees to make within
And sentences to construct

This is where I live
This is where I live

I am here
I cannot fathom the want
I am here
I see things as they are
To be
In the midst of things
I stand on the precipice of nature
And know
That to see again
Is to have my life enthralled

I am in love
With whatever it is that keeps me yearning
But I must stop
And take recompense at the stars
And here I will be the one who does not shirk

Hoping

That that the trees in twilight
Will have the distance covered
And the belief that the stars
Are here to help
I will fashion myself a new speed
And have done with the tendrils that bind

And here
Where I linger over the cover
I will be the silence
And the draft of soft glow
Will enter at its own time

And then
When we ride again
There will be nothing to hold us back
And when we arrive
A great celebration

There are things which the moon has forgone
As there are things which the sky has reneged
In the dream
There is more than this
In the stream there blows a might
When we come
There will be rejoicing
In the distance there is a lovely song
What have we heard
But all that is
What have we learnt
But all that is
I feel strong
Stronger than I ever have
And here I will stay
To where the suns shines
Before disappearing over the horizon

What in the centre is the boldness we seek?
It is here
Where dragonflies weep
It is here
Where the sentence buckles

Dark cloud White cloud Dusk Sandstone Volume 1

And the new need we have
To saddle the stars
Is once again translucent

I will only be what is
And here
Where we send
Our letters to the front
We will come again in the middle of something stranger

What is it we seek?
It is the farrowing of brows
And the distance that never speaks

I love this thing
It is what I was born to do
But what of the redress
That has the falconer in tears?
It is us
As we seek once again for new news to bring

There seems a riposte here
That comes in delighted night
Be the tune
And I will be the lullaby
Be the sense
And I will be the nonsense

You are, in every respect,
A likeness to the window
And that is what I must call you

In the depths of the languished insistence
There are fields that have no ilk
No tiredness that has fortitude
No belonging like this
I will be
And then delight
Be
And then delight
Be and then sing the carolling might

Paul Fearne

To sleep once again

I see you
Placated endeavour
I see your source
And know you to be that which binds
But here
Where we trumpet
There will be time

What is there left
Until the rain of the sea
Fills us all?
It is more than we could ever had imagined
And more than we could have hoped

I tire
And then
Like magic
I rouse
Until only sleep remains
I have been there
And then found myself wanting
The most solemn of times

What is there left
Until seas part?
What is there left?

The tutelage I find
Appealing
The tutelage I find
From ancient shores
In my time
I have buried myself in books
And learnt much
But something more must ensue
At each book that finds its way
To a reader
And here
I can find my way
Amongst new stars

New feathers
In new hats
And then
Discover once again
That life is a testament
And history will glean
Its senses
On new types of drive

 I have found
In my travels
That the world isn't round
It is oblong!
Perhaps a deceit of the senses?
Perhaps a new found truth?

When I come for you
Oh night
I will know you to be kind
And here
Where the trumpet blasts its loudest
I will never let go
I know you to be a friend
And my love for you is pronounced

You are the one
You see as far as autumn day
As long as the wisps of mist on a country walk
You
Are
The
One

And here
Where I have walked so often
I see pipers
And dreams of the living
I see sand
That has never known a footprint
And here
I will come

And believe once again
That the journey
Never ends

There is a place
That feels no flying grace
And here
Where the noise is palpable
I will lunge into things
Before the shock has set in
And the jezebels wilt to their mass
There is danger here
But only if we let it

The systematic sense
Of all that ever was
Is here now
Where enemies become friends
And we are left to see the day
For what it is

What do we see
When the light is gone?
We see ourselves
In morning garb
And then
When the newness of the day
Harbours all that is
There is time
To lay back
And feel us thronging
Through the streets
And through the airy expanse
Where a multitude of birds
Have been sent
To carry us away
And into the beyond

The same is always said
Of this, the march hare
In its life
It comes to the challenges of the dark

Dark cloud White cloud Dusk Sandstone Volume 1

And overcomes

And here
Where the distance never matters
There will be the sound of longing
As it travels up our spines
To that distant place
That has only the syncopation of travesty
Yet to be fulfilled

There are now
In this forest
Times to rest
But otherwise
It is all out activity
And a breath of air

I said yes
For dear Oscar's sake

There are times
That are here for labouring
There are times that are here for frivolity
And when we are through
May we all feel rest
It is such a mighty thing we do
To live
The things we do
The things we don't do
And here
With a mandate for change
We love
And in this motion
The too and fro of fate
We settle into something greater
And something that has at is base
The needs of a whole generation

What is this for
This need to be entrenched?
Entrenched in what?

In the living sense that is all of life
We come
And then are given to life
What is life?
It is there
It speaks
In whatever voice in encounters
Here is life
And here is us

The simplicity of things to come
Will be the thing that intrigues us

What can we believe in?
What can we say that doesn't hurt?
I have spent a life being
And to be
Is to flee
Flee the barbs
That send us scurrying
What is life, I ask again?
Barbs
And harrowing adventure

I have not forgotten my lot
It stands as a guard
That only lets me live
In small moments
Have you seen the tether?
Have you seen its wroth?
I have
And it stirs
The blood to boiling departure
Be sure
We will not fight

There are times
That need no introduction
There are wishings
That hold no fear
And when we see aright

There will be more
Than we ever hoped

The changing of the guard
Does not mean a dismissal
It only means
That we try that bit harder
To be ourselves
In the thick of it

What in this life
Have I not been privy to?
What
In this way
Do the shards of feeling
Never believe
I love the sound the sea makes
This is sure
But what of the rest?
The rest
That cannot be believed
In every sense of the word

The hoary insolvency
Of the last
Is not what it should be
And here
We will be again

The seeming intransigence
Of the night
Is something we must not encounter
We seethe
And in this motion
Know beauty
And all her might

In the delectability
Of the contrite
See ourselves
And know

Paul Fearne

That the well-wishes
Of a thousand days labour
Will here
Be the
One
To be true

I have found
That when we come anew
There will be at odds
The seeming delight
Of the whetstone
As she comes
It tethers of commitment

I love what is here
I write
And capture in words
This phenomenon:

Dark cloud White cloud Dusk Sandstone

And here
Where we see the most
I will love
For the last time

And when we see ourselves in the darkness
There will be a tried and true
Thing to say
And here
We must see ourselves again
Before it is too late

The feeling of the repartee
Is enough to quiet us
And when we see
The daylight between the trees
It will be as if
It is our first time to see the dawn
Believe me
It could not be truer

There needs to be a footing
In this place of dreams
A place I can sing
I dreamt last night
Of the former in these things
And it was a delight to see
Such fortitude
In the density
Of the searing light

And now
When I sit to write these words
I have at my side
A new book
It tells of adventures had
And new beginnings
And ways to be true

This is my guide
And my newness
And all that shall be

This is what I say to you
Do not be the one who lingers
Do not be the one who divests
Be the one who says
With no uncertainty
I will be
Like no other

And here I say to you
Be in the midst
Conquer with your being
Let it rise up
And be the tune that never was

Where we stand
There is nothing
Where we sit
There is nothing

And by 'nothing'
I mean everything

Can we even stand to be
What is the utmost?
I hope so
And here
Where the landfall gives respite
I will write
And know myself to be a troubadour
Of the highest inflection

The sense we have
That life is the thing that binds
I will have it
Pure
And then let it go
On pinions of last desire

You are here
As I am here
We wait
Until the danger is past
And then come again
Until we have no more might left
I sing to you
My long lost love
You would have hated these words
But they are enough

I sense a victory
In the wind
The wind chases
But what do we do?
We search
And search again
Until we can no longer search
(and then again)

The weather here
Is nice to the touch
It closes in

And then departs
As much couldn't be said
Of Shelly
On the Don Juan
On that ill-fated lake
A squall came
And then
History

New now
Newer than ever before
I reach into the abyss
For these words
And they come
With time to spare

The seemingness of the dark
Is all a charade
It is light
All the time
And here
Where the forest knows its journey
There will a feather
That floats down
On leaves unknown
And chances untaken

You are one to see
The things that are aright
And in the fledgling grace
That has happenstance as its guild
There will be the one who dreams
And dreams often

In the midst of departure
There is always a sound
It comes in waves
And knows not when to stop
It has a beauty to it
The beauty of the unknown
And all that is

There are times
When the dream burgeons
And times
When it slightly deflates
But here
Where the dream is at its height
There will come
New hope
And the wildest of fortuitous walkings

This is how it goes
One step
Two steps
Linger
Three steps
Fall
And here we have life
It all it grace

To be the one who never shirks
This is the key
It weathers
And darkens
But we never give up
And what is the seeming
Of giving up
Is
Not
So

Is there more?
I hope so
Is the midst of this embrace
There comes a unicorn
Through the mist
And then turning right
Here
We can see more
Than we ever have

The silence is a trait

Of the feeling we once had
To straddle the stars
And be in tune with the sea

I put myself there
So I can believe again
That life is virtuous
And things have a sense to them

Be in tune
With the ebb of the sea
Be in tune
With the fire that burns
Be in tune with the nightly august
And then come to play
The sand is washed away

In the weave
There is a nest
In the wondering
There is a vest
Come and play
We are here to stay
And then
We will be no more
And have the will
To say, I will

In the distance
I see a lark
It says to me
'Be the one who stays'
And I have heard its call
And I will
On one condition
That I be the one who listens

This temptation
To be the best
Is enough
To ride through the streets

Without the scaffolding that lowers brows
And hear
What is for
And what is blessed

In times of sorrow
We have life
It slings and barbs
But here is one thing
Life
I have seen many things
Heard many things
And this I know
There is no hurt that can break the human spirit
Impossible

And now
When the harp is singing
I will find you
Asleep
But not on a horse drawn carriage
I see you
As you sleep
I see you
And know you to be content
That is what I wanted
And here it is
Magical

What do we see
When we look up?
We see the clouds
(dark cloud, white cloud)
We see the sky
We see the stars
We see the moon
We sometimes even see the horizon
And here
Where so much is said
We come again
In new forms
And new fashions

And we hold ourselves aloft
And tell our grandchildren
That time is nothing but a ghost
And what we have
Is solace
Solace to do what we please
And solace to launch into things
Solace to reach into the abyss
And pull out the nothing that retains there
And all we will have left
Is the dreams of our forbears
And the nightly sprinkling
Of dust on ancient mantle pieces
And the sound of sparrows in the garden
As they teach their children
That suffering is not a thing
It can be overcome
And in the end
Done away with

You should not be close to the fire
It rages
But we all have protective garb
That help shield us
And then
When the belief
That the stars are here in all their glory
Subsides
There will be more
Than we could have hoped for
In tune
Yes
And no
Be the one who burns
And you will not burn brightest
But you will find love
And more than is wanting

This is the time
We must steel ourselves
We wait

On the ramparts of another dawn
Another chance to be

And here
Where the noise is like a harvest
We trunch in new gear
And have vestibules to guide us

The chance we have now
Is like something we never saw
It heals
As it evokes
It knows the sustenance that contains us
Is a thing to be treasured
And when
The like minded
Are here
They say to us
'You look like your father'
And then
When we dismiss them out of hand
They say to us
'You look like your mother used to'
And that placates us

What is more
(He says with a roar)
Is that the tune on the lyre
Is enough to bend the dawn
To new heights
And new depths
But what depths does the dawn reach?
Its one travel is up
Below
There is the machine
That pushes the dawn upward
And it is deep

The longing we feel
Is just another delay
A delay in what?
In the seeds of turning that shine the brightest

Dark cloud White cloud Dusk Sandstone Volume 1

And here
Where the noisome and the bold
Have their sand covered in silk
Here
The wishing of angels in waiting
Come in their merriment
Show due care
And you will be rewarded
Be the one to insight
And the noise will be great
I have found
That when the need is righteous
There can nothing other than this
I labour under the tutelage
And know deeds to be great

What we see
Are the shards of a former belief
What we find
Is something more than we had hoped

In the sentence
Lies invigoration
In the draft that comes
Receptacles
Receptacles of what
Of the wind as it races
And here
Where we find hope
There comes a new mass
That is all we hoped

There is a chance
That the longer we believe
The longer we will have our say

Be in the midst of things
Come into the tribulation
And know your release

What we always remember

Is that the time that is given us
Is enough to fill twenty volumes
And here
Where the sand does not move
I will move
And have the daylight to guard me
From all that comes

 Inside every one of us
Is the new and the old
Let us believe in the new
But hold the old
As a bastion
Of light
And commiseration

I have known many things
And where I write
I have some insight
To be the one who listens
Here I will come
And know myself to be an ancient bard
That believes in fate
But has more beside him

This time
The table has been turned
Upside down
And roundabout

And then
When we least expect it
Light
And all that will be

You are the favoured
As I am the down cast
You are the one who bites
But I have no say

What do you say
When night is here?

Dark cloud White cloud Dusk Sandstone Volume 1

I am now in a righteous mood
But the things which call
Are greater than any of us

 Come what may
I will continue

Here, where the sky has never been so bright
I light a fire
To remind me
Of the fire within

And when we traipse again
Along long forgotten roads
I see myself in you
And know that I can only write of one of us
But there are a few words I can say

The night is here
But what of the day?
She is gone
Gone to that other place
Have I been sad?
I know I have been wished well
In many things
But enough of this
Indeed

And now
Where we sit for hours
I know the time to start is upon us
We must gather our rose petals
And have the sense to man the barricades
And see into them
What we must

There is a hope here
That has no time
There is a nuance to things
I just cannot grasp
What do we do then?

We move forward
In hope
And fear

What do you fear
My departed?
I have no fear
Now that you are gone
I only have one thing
And that is the tempest
She rages
And brings me low
But I feel content
To watch myself
From the safety of the harness
But this must go to
And here
Where we stand upright
I will not let go
Of anything

This is it
The one troubadour
Left
In a wild land
We cannot be the ones to leave
We must be the ones who rattle
And here
I know my fate
I belittle the stagecoach
And know that the sound of the fire
Is not mine

What do we settle on?
The newness of a fading light
And here
Where we trudge ever onward
I know that this is my last
And never being one to be
I let be
And see the sun turn

In the forest
There is a new burning
It follows labyrinths untold
And where we see ourselves anew
Here we will see something more
We will see the turning
Of an earth
That has no knowledge of its birth
And there send its touch
Into lands uncharted
I love this
But how do we see it through
We do not
And find that thing in the middle
Instead

I know not what to say
I have said it all
And when we come for the night
We will know ourselves to be the sands
Of this very time

The trope is right
But what of the discomfort?
Here we lean a little closer to the fire
And know ourselves to be harsh

But what of this?
Does it matter if we see the distance as a thing to be
forgotten?
This matters not
There are no more weaves in the jungle
No more winding treasures that belie the need we have
I look like a man who has had adventures
Adventure
This is the key
I sense
What is the upholding of all that is
And here I will not be
And only descend on travellers dreams
There will be time

There will be time

I will hear nothing of it
That we should be lingering
In the outskirts
And here
Where we guess the most ardent passions
There will be life
And all that can be

And now
The silence comes in tow
It sees more than can be seen
And lets linger
The fortune of bravery
As it hurtles past
In strange
Translucence

The tutelage of forever
Is here
It tells of the lingering sense
We have that the dawn will be here
When we are least apt to feel it
There are more things
In this world
Than can be hinted at
By the trace and the delivery
In the song I sing
I test new ground
I come for more than is possible
And I see more
Than rights the way

Can there ever be
More than this?
Can the stars tinkle even more brightly?
Can the forest glade be even more beautiful?
This we must trace
When the nuances of the sun
Shine on untold sublimities
Here

We will only linger
Our journey is up
And through
And towards
And when the dance comes
We will shine
That mighty sheen
That is of the desert sun
And the moon
Whose eagle is the light
And the source

What say you?
Do we dance in the fabric of togetherness?
Or shoot through to isolation?
That are not questions easily answered
Each has its too's and fro's
Fro's are nightly
Too's are in the melting pot which is forever

There are new turns
And less than that
There are optimal things
Which have nothing to say
And here
Where the night is at its height
There comes a raging light
That dismisses the sea
'FOR WANT OF ADVENTURE'
Would you believe it

The most we can say
To placate the sand of the sea
Is that we were there
When the sun rose
We were there
When the rain came
Over the horizon
And through the trees
We were there
When the lake was filled

And the new black of the sky
Was given to the multitudes
And here
Where the beliefs are well-polished
There will be a chance to dream
And a chance to be the one
Who dances
All through the solstice

What is in me
Is in you
What we find when we wake
Wakes us all
And here
Where we sleep
There are new songs
And new chances to be

I love the race
It sends me forward
And into what awaits
I see now
There is nothing
In the fibre of things
To appease the wantings
That are our pain and pallor

What do you do
When the daylight has a new need?
You saddle up your horses
And try once again
For this or that
For here
Or there
And then realise
That the journey is a syncopated musing
That knows no sound

And when the dance is done
There will come a shard of light
It will know itself
As you know it

As all of life
Just one shard of light
And it is all there
And here we will find it
In our very bones
In our very being
In our very happiness
And here we will be
To stand the test
And know ourselves to be
Everything we wanted
And more

I am here
Where wind and sea meet
In unison
And where the sea
Doesn't move
There will be a love
So grand
That it sparks
All that is
And into what awaits

 What do you do
When the telescope is trained on the stars
And your new found love
Is basking in the glow?

I say to myself
Can I do more?
And here
Where solace meets insistence
There is the way beyond
Which is not the way here
But a way there
And new found belief
That the night
Is not
All that is

The sense we have
That when we are at the helm
There is nothing more to say

The density of the commiserations
Abhors the void
And here
Where the plants of the well-spring
Are in there might and night
There will be something else
That has the newfound longing
As its rectilinear shoulder
Here
We must let go
And love where we have loss
And dream that the album of daisies
Is enough
To get us where we won't to go
And help us believe again
That life is for the adventurous

What haven't we believed in?
Neither this
Nor that
Nor any thing worthy of a worn out soul

And here
Where the trajectory of love
Is at its zenith
There will be more to say
Than ever before

I hear you say
'I am in need of something'
And I ask
'What is that?'
And you say
'Everything'
And what do I say to that?
I let that go into the ether
And watch it settle there
Like a breeze that has nothing to say

Or a sun that has no planet

Where are the ruminations of the stars?
Have they had their say?
Have they been to the bottom?
And then to the outside
Have they seen the withering glance?
Have they known what it means to suffer?
Have they truly been in love?
I say that things cannot get more licentious
But this is now, not ten years ago
But yes, we harbour no regrets
And do not fathom the boundaries of the divisive
What of the here and now?
It will find its way
And then be true once again
Not before too long at least

What is it we seek?
Do we seek fame?
Do we seek desire and all it can bring?
Do we seek love?
Do we seek anything in this world?
It all fades

But what of the transparencies of youth?
Forever young?
Soon to be saddled with life's yoke

There can never be anything more than this
The right here and now
That is all we can live for
To be directly here
And now
And then tail away
Into the shores of the morrow

What is this thing called belief?
It is the rallying point
And the tendering home
It is the list and not the heather

It comes it tropes
And does not seem to be
When looked for
Lo, it is not found
But we all need its feather
And its bow
Where do we find ourselves
When belief is in the outskirts?
When find ourselves here
At this point
Writing away
Despite fear, and with no favour
The writing begins
And never stops

What is in the depths, I hear you ask?
It is nothing more than everything
And nothing
Depending on your point of view
It is the surest measure
And the guarding moment
It is the want of leisure
The auburn sun
It is the window that looks
And the soldiers that see
(and who are at sea)
What is this, I hear you ask?
Ask no more
That can be no more explanation
Only this
…
And then
(silence)

Happening
Here
Happening
There
What is happening?
The shores of the sea have elongated
And do not know when to stop
And here

Brethren
There are the seeds of a larger turning
Fathoming up the mainsails
And having the sound of life
Caught in our throats
What is this sound
The sound of life?
Listen
Listen now
It is here
And where you are now

Whether we float
Or hear the brew
Is not what the sands of time
Can decide
Here
The withal
And without
Is here in the heather
That has no space to chew
Or fat to harness
For another feast
Another festive degree
That has the light
And the song
Alone on its side
And with care
It goes
(beyond the pale)

The sentience of the pall
Derides great fervour
From the favour of the night
Who sits here
In bastions of desire?
But where do we sit
Where we shan't lose the tips and all
Of all and the beautiful?
We sit here
Near the building I was brought up in

And here I wonder
Where is the fight
That we need now?
To transform us into the tallest of men
And here truncate the arbour
That is more than a feather
And less than desire can tell of
Here
Be restrained
There is more to say

What has happened
To the sun and its light?
Where do we now get our solidity from?
What is the harrow and the whistle?
Who draws us on in times of need?
We are here still
And we placate to find sustenance
What is more
We weld shut the gate
That has let in so many
We do this
Out of heart
And new ways to be
But what of this
The dark
We will not be attentive
To the ceiling and the misnomer
We will get on with glee
In our hearts
And the robe of Achilles
On our shoulders

Our bones
Our bones
Where have they gone?
In what direction
Blind and steep
In what mass do they co-exist?
In what elation do they fidget?
Be the raga-muffin
And there will be cries

Be the Holland and the field
And we will come for more

What is more
Is that the sense the clouds have
That the horizon will not stay
Is enough to soothe the sire
Of the day
And give back what the penultimate has been
Ready to fear
And hear
Once again
There are the dreams of a firefly
As it arches in and out
Of the true sense of duty
That we find
When we pick up the mass of old books
And put them into storage
That has no light at all
Or draw strings to let any in

There circles around
And around
The cape of good hope
A mighty demi-urge
That enters in
As we gain strength
And know that the evening will only last
If we let it
And here
Where the two sides of the same coin
Evenly split
There will be a rectilinear array of surprise
That will be the thing that shocks
And lets us breath again
And again
That deeper breath
That is home

Paul Fearne

There can be nothing greater
Than the mist
As it spills down the hillside
As the dawn sheds its light through the scene
And there is no wind
Not a feather
No sense of the here or now
Not a climbing branch
But climbing vines
The mist passes through them like a viper
And then comes to rest
I see you
Oh past
I see you now
What has been will never return
What has come to pass
Has indeed passed
And here
Where we see again
Deliverance

What have I said
A thousand times
The air we breath
Is nothing
The human spirit is all
As the climbing to the highest point
As the descent to any safety
As new points of sadness
That uplift in their sadness
And here
There can be no more
No more trying
No more staying
No more wanting to be this or that
The corporate
And the demi-urge
Rule only the smallest part
Of a much greater realm

What is the newest thing
The rainbow has found?

Is it the sympathetic gregariousness
Of a want and a troubadour
That has the smile of a thousand faces?
Maybe so
And when we see the well-spring
Of a thousand places
Here we will shriek 'hark, who comes there'
And be better placed than ever
To see the lark and the weather
All melding into one
That has as its tone
The shallowness of the rind
So be with us
New sights
Be with us
And be the one who never sees
But only through the mist
Of our own devising

What is this we say
When the rainbow has not slept
And the diligence of the dusk
Is near at hand

Here I will not shirk
Here I will only be a sayer of languishing dreams
And when there is enough
There will be something more
Something that comes in spades
Onto the lonesome scene
And begs to differ
Here the dance is at its peak
We have made friends
With all those
We might see as rollicking
But not
Only now
We shall see

What is the sense
Is not in the nonsense

Paul Fearne

But what is the nonsense
Is nothing more than all

Come now
Be placated
There will be time
To see the weather through

What are these barbs
That send us thinking anew
They are the barbs of life
As they see through the battlements
And into the field
The field of what though?
The field of laughter
And commiseration

There comes a time
In everybody's life
When the meeting
Of strange metals
Is enough to drive one to distraction
And here
Where angels meet
There will be guidance
And a margin of salt
To rattle away the cobwebs
Of a thousand nights labour
And here
Where we fall
More of the love
We once felt

Have the strength
To carry the tray
And your world will be yours
And all manner of things
Will be righted
Come now
It couldn't be so sure
But what of the nightingale
And her stamp?

She is here
In spirit at least
And here in body as well
We must not disturb her
Until the very end
And then we will find her singing
That great song
And we will not contain our joy
Not curtail our spirits

What do we do
When the lights begin to fade?
We gather up our rose petals
And have them by our side
We point to the dawn
And say a loud 'Yes'
We know what forms
Are the basis for this dream
So we dream away
And let fate take her course
This is the only thing we can do
And we must do
To be sure
We adjust the visor of our helm
And carry on
Up the slope
And into forever

The time is right
The time is now
I will write this book
And these books
Until testing times are through
And then I will gather myself
For more adventures ahead
You see, there is never end to this
Until we depart for one last time
And here
Where the nest of all our making
Is dawned on summer silk
Here

Paul Fearne

Motion will protect
And distance will no longer have its appraisal
Be sure
There can be more
More if we like it
Less if we don't

Come down to the tow
We are swimming in silk
And here
Where the metered rhythm
Of every poem that has ever been written
Is allowed a reading by a living poet
And the joy
And the feathered mass
The un-truncated joy
The seeming impossibility of it all!
Alack, there is more
More to come in this place of sentential wonder
There will be more than we have hoped
And here
We will find it
Joy
And all that she shall bring

I am with the sea
She is scurrying me
I have held my own up
And know that the dance is yet to come
And here
Where there are more to things
Than meets the eye
There will be terror
In the eyes of none
There will be swinging from lamp posts
And more than this
There will be happiness
And a long lost sentience
There will be hope
And all that will come to pass
It comes to pass
In the flash of an eye

And knows itself to be truth
As we ever perceived it

'What is in the window?'
I hear you ask
It is not worth the look
But look none the less
Look
And have your fill
Such sights are for the bold and the daring
Have as much now as you wish
Tomorrow will bring another day
Of fun and adventure
And all that should be gotten
In bags of silken ash
And where there are the marks of the furthest shore
We will go
On an adventure to find them
And not know which way is up
And not know which way is down
But to know
Which way is horizontal

Foraging in the mass of things
I find a secret passageway
It directs me to follow it
And so I do
And when we are at the end of its sloping corridors
We find a door
I slowly open the door
And look through
It is the sea!
Covered in a mist of Time's making
I close the door
And go back down the corridor
I will always know where this is
And when I need to replenish my senses
I come back here
And open my door
And look out to sea
And the mist which covers it

Paul Fearne

What is this thing
That barks in the night?
Is it the land
Which in covering all
Covers nothing?
Is it the sky
Which
In covering most
Covers least?
I am at the road
And can see clearly
I am at that furthest point
And can only see the back of me
Where is the landing?
I here you ask
It is not for us to tell where it is
But only for us to tell

What is there left to say?
We have spoken all the words that can be spoken
We have winged through space and time
And have not had the new need devised for us
Nor the wellbeing of a compass
Drawn to our own specifications
Here
There are more things
Than can ever be counted
By any counting machine
Devised

What is more
We have not seen the back of the mirror
It stands upright
So we can see ourselves in the front
But the back remains a mystery

When we come once again
To that misty clime
We will know beauty
And all that she has to say
And here
Where sand is no longer the partner

There will come a ringing
A sound that vaults as it vaunts
And here
Where we find no other life
There will be truth
And singing
And all the ghostly apparitions we could want

Now that we are in the throes of desire writ true
We will not shirk our responsibility to be with time
As we winds down the ages
And seek ourselves again in love

There are new things
Here
To discover
We never spent enough time looking down at our feet
As we walked

The new things are ancient things
It is a surprise we haven't seen them before
But they come now
To our sense of sight
They are the shape of shells
Not sea shells
But shells of the sky
They litter the roadway
And when the road turns
They turn
And on the footpath
Shells
And more shells
This is how it goes

But what are these shells made of?
They are made of the silver lining of clouds
And the innards of rainbows
As they trace through the sky

And now they litter the road way
And the footpaths

Where we all walk
And a great crunching sound erupts
From every step
'Crunch, crunch, crunch' the sound goes
But we are not shocked
Or perturbed
There can be more of this
Whenever we like

The sense we have
That the surrogate to the stars
Is the guiding force
Of all that is
And all that will be

And then
When we have met our fill of things
We can recast the statue on the road
That tells of courageous and heroic deeds
We can simply recast it
To resemble us
And we will be of bronze
Doing courageous and heroic deeds
Why don't we anyway
Without a statue to honour us
Just let a filter of the courageous and heroic
Fill us
And then
Off we go
To action!

There is all we could ever want
Right here
In front of us
Right now
And here
Where time has been kind
We will believe the kind of things
That have no prayer for
And no respite for
And here
Where we stay together

There is the filings of rulers
That have no partiality
And no need to be
The troubadours of the past
But of the now
We will be guided by past things
But find out self in the now, to be sure

What do we say to ourselves
When the nucleus has broken free
And the time it takes us to
Sing to each other
Is more like a sail in the wind
Than a wind in the sail
So how do we say
What we feel
When all that is left
Is the new
And the old
Be here
My favoured beginning
You are the one who seeks not
The one you feels not
And the one who builds the courage
To say
Enough
And then move on
And through
And into

Whether we sit
Or walk
Or swim
Or engage in any sort of motion
Or immobility
Here we will find our life
Not here
Not there
Not in the wind
Not in the sand
On any beach

But in motion
(or immobility)
We find ourselves
Here

There are chances in the dark
And chances in the light
I come or this chance
As it is my life
I come for this chance
As the wind sears through my bloodied fist
(it is my blood)
I come for this chance
As I sing towards the morrow
And all that she will bring
I sing
And sing
And never stop
Never tire
So I take that chance
And see where it leads me
Forward, inwards, outwards backwards

What is most at stake
Is our sanity
How do we rely on ourselves
When to do so
Brings us so much suffering
How do we rely on that which is unreliable?
All we do is pretend
Pretend we have the perfect life
And in pretending, make real
Manifest the perfect life
From way up above
To down below
To the bottom of the sea
And back again
Through the clouds and the sky
To the stars
And here rest
The perfect life

Here we stand then
On the precipice of something new
What is so new about this place that stands out?
A good feeling, a dash in the dark response to ever
burgeoning life
Here we find time to settle
And know that when we are through
There will be time for reflection
And a little bit of homecoming cheer
What is there left
That should make us sound so hoary
It is the feather in my cap
And the snow beneath my feet
These are the things which lift me
Hold me
And eventually carry me away
What have I found here
But all
What have I found here
But all that is

But what is love?
It is about abandonment
And an element of deception
Some seek it
Some flee from it
Many just have it happen to them
When they least expect
And where there is to
There is fro
And where there is this
There is that
Love
The great mystery
Could it happen to you?
It could indeed
But it is not the panacea
Many think
So take your risk
Something to think about

Paul Fearne

There are places that do not bite
There are places that whisper our names
Until the breeze blows to pleasantness
There are places
There are places
There are places have the solstice as the dream
There are places that have the new
And the old
Together
On the one shelf
There are places
There are places
Do we believe in the need of one?
Yes we should
And here find our release
In the nomenclature of tomorrow
And all she shall bring

The one thing we should do
Is not to sit through the levity
Of a thousand nights inaugurated
We should rather stand
And participate in the throng
And here
Where we find most our time to be
There will be a mighty release
That will taste stranger than a pickled ham
And in the midst of it
The sound of fighting in the distance
Can this be real?
Can this be real?
Yes it can
Oh yes it can

What is said
Here
Is more than enough
To fill countless volumes
And what is said
In the time in between times
Is enough
To fill countless volumes

And here
Where we stand again
And again
For another chance at happiness
And find that our chances are
Wet with morning dew
They glisten
In the air
And see themselves to be things of unknown disposition
And when we arrive
We really arrive!

In time to see it
I let go of my posture
And slouch
On the first seat I see
And here
Where the ragamuffin and the train
Circle each other for life
More personified that ever
There can only be this
In every page
Of every book of history
This is all that is
And all that shall be
But wait
Can we note change things
For our own happiness?
Yes we can
And here we will
Bend time
And be one with history

Having a chance to just be
I reminisced that the world was a spectacle
And from the outside
Looking in
You could not determine the full extent of the world's
suffering
A lot of it would be invisible to your sight
People walking around

Not seemingly in suffering
But suffering never the less
And when the boat is in the distance
We will run for it
And know our chance is safe
And our suffering at an end
And here we will take life on its own merits
And feel how the simplicity of forever
Knows how to trace a circle
From the books
On Rembrandt

On the window sill
A hand
On the ground
Two feet
In the middle a person
Someone in side
Lifts them up, and now they are warm
There can only be one tale like this
And it is this tale
It is the tale of two halves
A tale of the long and the short of it
Where we get stuck
Is not where we begin
But where we end
I will not suffer in vain
That is my motto
I will not suffer in vain

The seething mass
That is our hearts is not for the sail
Nor the rectilinear
It is for the treading of solemn rights
That have not sense of the vertical
And the waste
Here
Where the sand is coloured
And the new whistling we have found
Is nothing we should feel spite for
I have found more in these pages
Than anything I have read so far

That is okay
For when the stable door is left ajar
We will sneak back in
And shut it
Before it is too late
Before the horse
Finds its way
Outside

The newness of the self
Finds its way somewhere close
But it is an illusion not to be encountered
So do not fear!

Come, be true
Come and be that things that has not spite
Be that thing that has no feeling nor derision
And all else will be yours
What do you say to that
Monsieur?
There will be more times for discussion
Than we ever felt possible
And here
Where I come
To the post
I will find you
And all will be well

What is there to do
That does not seem odd?
 What is there to do
That does not put a right
In the right place?

What is more
There is never a place to be seen
When to be seen
Has itself been seen
A thousand times
A million times
What do we do then?

We cast ourselves into the abyss
And travel for a thousand days
And in that time
We see ourselves a thousand different ways
In a thousand different modes
And here we rest
And show ourselves to be at rest
This is the solution

Which citadel do we mean here?
Which place to call home
A home amongst the clouds?
A home beneath the sea?
A home on the line of the horizon?
Yes all of them
And more

There are traces of togetherness
Amongst the debris
Traces of togetherness
And then what is more
Traces of the togetherness
Of time
And her ilk

What is seen through this castle window
Is nothing else
But all
What can be seen out of this castle window
Is all
And now that the picture is hanging on the wall
We can make finite of the infinite
And see ourselves
As one with all
And all that is
Think about this
When the time we have is short
Think about this
When the little bit of hardness colours the day
We are all
And this much is certain

Dark cloud White cloud Dusk Sandstone Volume 1

What is this mist
That gathers around
Is it the mist of ages
As they curl around our feet?
If it was such
There is much knowledge there
You can read of such
In gold lettering that the mist has contained within it
It is a such a brilliant sheen
It almost glows
And written on these tablet like mist constructions
Are all manner of things
Ethics
Belief
Wisdom
Compassion
And all very small
One must bend over to see
But then it can be read
With utmost precision

The utmost
I will take you there
Flying over
Under
In between and through
Here is the life
And the wedding
And the new start of the day
Here is the new found land
The tether
The wanting
The travelling
Have we found what we were looking for
Up there
In the trees above
What is above
Is below
What is in between
Belies explanation

I will run to you
Oh fate
I will run to this very spot
Again
And again
And see you at work
There are differences in the way we speak
But much can be said of both of us
Fate
Oh fate
Will you be the one for me?
Yes
And no
Yes, because we both are travellers
But no, because, well, no!

The life line we use
Everyday
Is enough to pull us back into the wreck
But where do we go from there?
We go inward
Deeply inward
And then through
And away we go
Back to life
Back to normalcy
And not a tear is seen
On any eye
That watches this progress
Completely gripping
Completely unbelievable
This race of ours
Completely gripping
This is what I say

Be the one who saves
This will be the figure
And all will follow
From this

The tempest has no might
Anymore

Or should I say
It has less might
The tempest is in the grass
It is in the trees
In the mountain tops
On the snow
On furthest places
And here
Where we look the most ardently
A figure of speech comes
And we say
Onwards

What is there in the dawn
That has us nearing completion?
It is simple
It is the night that has diminished
And the day that is just beginning
These two powerful forces
Are running away
With the heard and the sound

What can we give of ourselves
But all
What can we say to ourselves
But yes
And what is there left to be
But all that is
Be the one
I implore you

What has been tied
Can only be released
With a quill
That has written a book
This much I tell myself
Before I go to bed
And when I am there
Ah
The dreams that come
That are of such astounding beauty

That I hear not the sound of my own breathing
And in this deathful state
I go to the dreams of yore
And from there
Dream a solemn dream
Of the niceties of some adventures
And not others
And here I sleep
And be calm
Not before too long at least

What is waiting the sun?
It is the west
What is being in depth?
It is the sea, and her longing
What is the sign of life?
It is us, as we search again for higher ground

What can be said of us now?
Now that we have travelled so far?
It tells in the seam of things
That we shall be all we want
The withholding of daggers
Is not for us
We seek adventure
Without the fight
We seek more in the seam of things
Than ever before

What have we fought for?
Is it this?
Or that?
Was it more, was it....now
We have fought for the now
And we have found it
What a mighty thing
That feathers up to the dawn
In miniature gusts
And roundabouts
And here
Where we find the new steed
We harbour long hoped for dreams

Dark cloud White cloud Dusk Sandstone Volume 1

The now
The now
Before my unbelieving mind
We should be thankful
And we are

To be the ones that sink
Is not in us
To be the ones who raise up
Is more like us
But what is most like us
Is to be the ones who fly
To unknown heights
And this is where we will stay
Higher than any moon
For any planet
Higher than any star
To be seen from any vantage point
This is where we will stay

The longing we feel here
Is a longing well adjusted
Is crushed and thunders
Until we all wonder
What is this?
It is all that is

When we come to the conclusion of this song
We will know one thing
Language is for fun
And insight will never trouble reason
To be the one who is care free
Is not what we are after
To write, requires a right mental state
Brought on by a set of circumstances
The set consciousness to a heightened state

And here we must absolve ourselves of fun
And come up for air
The distraction of an age is at finest
And we will go to see it

Paul Fearne

One hand
Two hand
Three hand
Four

Here we go then
I am at the winter solstice
I wear my best jacket
Many people like this jacket
And I like it
It is splendid
There are many people at this place
Standing out the front of a winter castle
And here
Where the noise is great
A great thing occurs
The ground rumbles
And out rushes icy water
Very briefly, then gone
Some get wet, and go inside the castle to dry
But those of us who are still dry, stay to watch the sky
And it fades to stars
And all that winder has

I have known many things
Peace being one of them
But in my registry of feelings
There is nothing I haven't felt
From the great
To the small
To the in between

The gull flies straight ahead
Not knowing when to turn
It has travelled a long distance to get here
And knows that home is soon here
What is more
The distance never matters
The distance never matters

The distance never matters

And here
Where the dust has never settled
There are trees that have no bite
They are tall
And even grandiose
But bite they do not
And here
Where the dust has never settled
Trees that have no bite
Yes that's right
Trees that have no bite
And here we will be happy
Where the dust has never settled
Where the dust has never settled
Trees
Trees that have no bite

There are things that have in them
The very nature of the real
But they are not of this place
What we have here
Are traces
That gallop up
In infinitely tuned disposals
The things that bind us
Are the very things that set us free

In the middle of this malaise
There is truth
And here
Where we send our most ardent love
There be peace
Like we have never known it

The tendrils of desire
As many know
Are the things which keep us begging
But what of this life
This thing that we have persisted in our whole lives?
We are like more than we had ever hoped for

We must just look
And lo
We are here

The thing which dreams
Is the same thing that gives us hope
Yes
Hope
And all that we need

Be the one who says yes!
And the dangers will pass
I will liken myself to a pedestal
And you may place all you want on me
And here I will sing
And know my voice to be a thing that bleeds
Be in the middle I say
And life can never get better

There are things that are in the wind
And things that are outside it
What we find when we sail
Is that we have life
And this life is nothing other than all

I have travelled far on this wind
It blows in tempest blasts
And then is quiet
But who in their right mind would sail this journey?
Who would take this leap?
There is nothing left for me than to continue
I want so much more from life
But can it give what I want?
Yes it can
But in a way I cannot fathom

Be on the mast when the wind blows
And here
Where we come for what is right
I will know the passage to be a safe one

There are new found longings in the trees

They saddle up to the side of things
In an unreal manner
And send us to our knees
(but only for a short time, this is sure)
You see
We are used to the adventure now
(we must be ready for adventure at all times
It is what gives us our strength
And let's us see things clearly)

In the sense we have
We must be content to be
Rather than envelope
And the thing we see is all that is
In a single thing
Is this Blake's grain of sand?
We must see the world here
So we can rest
And be content with things

There is a dreaming
That we have always found comfort in
And here
Where we love to linger
We must have our last dream
And be ready for the sun as it floats higher than we ever
thought
The one thing I have heard
Is that happenstance is the goal of the mighty
Who are the mighty?
Beings who only exist in dreams
They are the ones who believe for us
And we thank them in our sleeps
For this
They themselves are thankful
And admire what we can be
And what we say
In times of the need
And the want
And here
Where we are the ones that shine

There can only be what we desire
And this is nothing
I will wait
Until I have found what I am looking for
It is close
Maybe now

I linger in the afterglow
Of this life and the next
I sense I will be that thing that has no recourse
To what has been past
But this matters little
For the present is all I have
It is here
I cast myself in bronze
And know
That that the present is what matters the most

I long for the grandeur of the afterglow
And here
Where mistletoe adorns all features
I will sing with my whole breath
There can only be things of beauty here
And when we sight with our unusual sight
There will come a dancing that has no ilk
In this or that
Be true
It is the way
Be in the training for now
And you will be prepared
I love this, I think
I love the too and fro of an unusual beckoning
Be here
I implore you
There will be nothing more to say

www.ingramcontent.com/pod-product-compliance
Lightning Source LLC
Chambersburg PA
CBHW022153080426
42734CB00006B/417